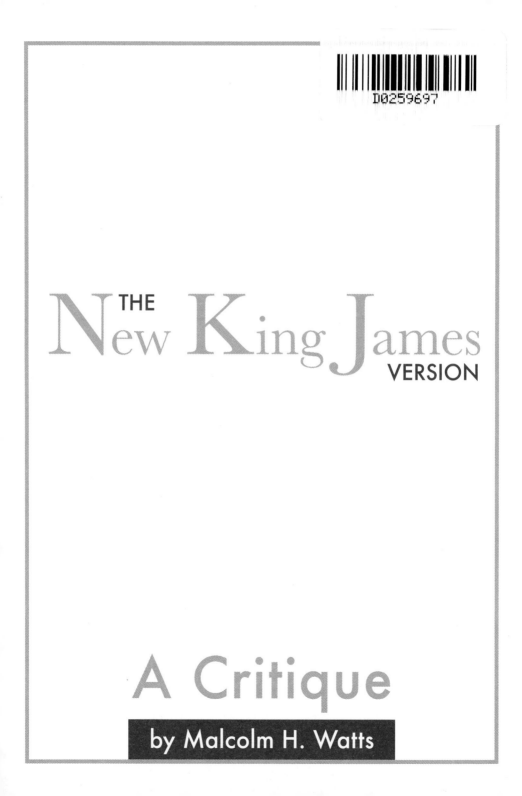

THE New King James VERSION

A Critique

by Malcolm H. Watts

ISBN 978 1 86228 357 2

© 2008 Trinitarian Bible Society
Tyndale House, Dorset Road, London, SW19 3NN, UK
Registered Charity: England 233082, Scotland SC038379

2M/05/14

The New King James Version: A Critique

Malcolm H. Watts

When this new translation of the Bible was published in the USA in 1982, the publishers, Thomas Nelson, stated that their aim was 'to produce an updated English Version that follows the sentence structure of the 1611 Authorized Version (AV) as closely as possible...to transfer the Elizabethan word forms into twentieth century English'.[1] The 'Preface' to the New King James Version (hereinafter NKJV) stated that the Old Testament would be a translation of the Hebrew Masoretic Text and the New Testament would be a translation of the Greek Received Text, the same Texts used by the AV translators in 1611.[2] This appeared to be a major improvement on many previous translations such as the New International Version, which is not based on the Received Text but is widely used in Evangelical circles.

However, there are serious problems with the NKJV.[3]

The Old Testament

It is made clear in the 'Preface'[4] that in translating the Old Testament of the NKJV reference was made to the Septuagint (the Greek translation of the Old Testament, c. 200 BC), the Latin Vulgate (a Latin translation undertaken by Jerome in AD 383), various ancient versions (presumably including such as the Aramaic Targums, dating from the Persian period, and the Syriac Version, approximately AD 60), and the Dead Sea Scrolls (Hebrew texts from pre-Christian and early Christian times, discovered in 1947).

There is evidence for use of these sources in the margins of the Old Testament. For example,

1

Genesis 4.8 has this note in the margin: 'Samaritan Pentateuch, Septuagint, Syriac, and Vulgate add *"Let us go out to the field"'*; Deuteronomy 32.8 has as a note on 'the children of Israel' the following: 'Septuagint, Dead Sea Scrolls *angels of God*; Symmachus [a revision of the Septuagint, approximately AD 180], Old Latin [exhibiting a pre-Vulgate text] *sons of God'*; Job 22.25 has 'The ancient versions suggest *defense*; Hebrew reads *gold* as in verse 24'.

The danger of such inclusions in the margin is that the reader is given the option of either taking the correct Masoretic reading or of deviating from it, following some non-Masoretic textual variant. This is surely undermining to the verbally inspired and Providentially preserved Word of God.

Furthermore, there are cases where such readings have become part of the text itself. For example:

■ In 1 Chronicles 6.28, וּשְׁנִי (*Vashni*), the name of Samuel's firstborn son, is changed to Joel after the Septuagint, Syriac and Arabic. He appears to have been called both names (see verse 33 and 1 Samuel 8.2), but there is no textual justification for the other name being included here.

■ Psalm 4.4 has רִגְזוּ וְאַל־תֶּחֱטָאוּ (*rigzu val-techetau*) which should read 'stand in awe, and sin not', but this is changed in the NKJV to 'be angry, and do not sin'. This seems to be both inaccurate and inappropriate (the Hebrew word means 'trembling'), and appears to follow the Septuagint and Latin Vulgate.

■ Obadiah 12 has בְּיוֹם נָכְרוֹ (*byom nacro*) 'the day that he became a stranger', which is changed to 'the day of his captivity' – despite a marginal note stating that this is 'Literally *on the day he became a foreigner*' – which loses the idea of estrangement, ruins the obvious climax throughout the verse, and once again appears to follow the Latin Vulgate.

Although accuracy is claimed for the NKJV, there are numerous Old Testament renderings which are simply erroneous or, at the very least, most misleading. We note the following:

■ Leviticus 19.16 – 'blood' (דָּם, *dam*) is changed to 'life', missing the whole point of the verse that 'tale-bearing' breeds strife and often leads to the shedding of 'blood' (see Ezekiel 22.9).

■ Deuteronomy 27.26 – omission of 'to do them' (although the words are in the Hebrew: לַעֲשׂוֹת אוֹתָם, *lasot otam*), which removes the proper sense of the verse.

- 1 Samuel 16.14 – change of רוח־רעה (*ruach-raah*, 'an evil spirit') to 'a distressing spirit' (also changed in verse 23 and 19.9).

- 1 Samuel 25.8 – יום טוב (*yom tob*, ' a good day'), is translated 'a feast day', which implies without any warrant that this was one of the regular feasts of Israel; it may mean no more than 'a happy day' or 'a day of rejoicing'.

- 2 Samuel 22.3 – 'the God of my rock' (צור, *tsur*) is wrongly rendered 'the God of my strength'.

- Psalm 30.4 – instead of 'the remembrance of his holiness', the NKJV has 'the remembrance of His holy name', which is not a translation but an interpretation since the Hebrew has 'holiness' (קדש, *qadosh*; see also 97.12).

- Psalm 33.15 – 'He fashioneth their hearts alike' is changed to 'He fashions their hearts individually', but the Hebrew (יחד, *yachad*) means that all alike are made by Him.

- Psalm 43.1 – 'Judge me, O God', in the sense of 'do justice for me' (שפטני, *shaphteni*), is translated 'Vindicate me', a rendering which goes beyond the meaning of the original. The word means no more than 'do justice in my case' or 'on my behalf' without necessarily presupposing a favourable outcome.

- Psalm 45.13 – 'The king's daughter *is* all glorious within' (כל־כבודה בת־מלך פנימה, *kal-kbudah bat-melek pnimah*) is changed to 'the royal daughter *is* all glorious within *the palace*'; although added in italics, the words 'the palace' are a totally unwarranted and unnecessary addition.

- Psalm 110.3 – 'Thy people *shall be* willing' is changed to 'Your people *shall be* volunteers', a most unhappy translation, particularly as the Hebrew (נדבת, *ndabot*) literally reads, 'Thy people shall be willingnesses'.

- Psalm 113.7 – 'the dunghill' (מאשפת, *meashpot*) from which men are raised, is improperly and weakly translated 'the ash heap', missing the point that men are sunk in moral degradation (see also 1 Samuel 2.8).

- Ecclesiastes 12.11 – 'the masters of assemblies' (literally, 'masters of gatherings' – בעלי אספות, *baale asupot*), is feebly translated 'the words of scholars' (although they admit in a footnote that this is 'Literally *masters of the assemblies*'), thus losing the idea of 'ministers' who are conveners and instructors of congregations.

■ Isaiah 1.27 – 'converts' is changed to 'penitents', but the Hebrew word (שׁוּב, *shub*) is commonly used to mean return, and in this passage it means 'her [Zion's] returners'.

■ Isaiah 7.16 – 'abhorrest' is changed to 'dread', whereas properly the word (קץ, *qats*) means 'loathe', originally associated with the feeling of nausea.

■ Isaiah 14.9 – 'Hell from beneath is moved for thee' is changed to 'Hell from beneath is excited about you', but the idea (רגז, *ragaz*) is that the spirits of the lost are 'roused' and not just a little 'surprised' to see the King of Babylon descending to that region.

■ Isaiah 61.3 – 'To appoint unto them that mourn' is changed to 'To console those who mourn', but the Hebrew word (שׂים, *sim*) certainly requires 'set', 'appoint', 'supply' or 'give'.

■ Jeremiah 1.17 – 'Gird up thy loins' (ואתה תאזר מתניך, *vatah tezor matneka*) is changed to 'prepare yourself', which is a departure from the original and an example of dynamic equivalence.

■ Lamentations 5.10 – The word 'black' (כמר, *kamar*) in the sentence 'our skin was black like an oven', is rendered 'hot', an unhelpful substitution. The Hebrew word, although not the common word for black, conveys the idea of growing hot and being scorched. In the change, the NKJV loses the idea behind the word, of being scorched so that the skin shows the effect of the exposure to the heat.

■ Ezekiel 5.17 – 'evil [רעה, *raah*, 'bad'] beasts' becomes 'wild', a meaning which it never has in the Hebrew.

■ Ezekiel 9.10,11 – 'I will recompense their way' is changed to 'I will recompense their deeds', but the Hebrew word (דרך, *derek*) means 'way' and is singular. Also, in verse 11 'reported the matter' (משיב דבר, *meshib dabar*) is rendered 'reported back', with the word indicating 'matter' omitted.

■ Ezekiel 16.46 – שׂמאל (*semol*), 'left hand', and ימין (*yamin*), 'right hand' are rendered 'north' and 'south' respectively, which may well be what is to be understood, but it is not what has been written in the Hebrew.

■ Daniel 8.21 – מֶלֶךְ (*melek*), 'king' is arbitrarily and inconsistently (cf. 7.17) changed to 'kingdom', but 'king' here appears to be used in a dynastic sense even as later in the verse it is used in a personal sense.

These comprise only a sample of the erroneous and defective translations in the NKJV as far as the Old Testament is concerned, but they are surely enough to warn – and indeed to alarm – sincere believers who desire to read and study a true and accurate version of the Holy Scriptures.

The New Testament

In further reading of the NKJV's 'Preface', written by its principal Editor, Dr A. L. Farstad, it becomes clear that he himself is not happy with the Received Text and actually endorses the so-called Majority Text. He writes elsewhere, 'Today, scholars agree that the New Testament textual criticism is in a state of flux. Very few scholars favor the Received Text as such, and then often for its historical prestige as the text used by Luther, Calvin, Tyndale and the AV. For about a century most have followed a Critical Text...which depends heavily upon the Alexandrian type of text. More recently many have

abandoned this Critical Text...for one that is more eclectic. Finally a small number of scholars prefer the Majority Text which is close to the Received Text except in the Revelation'.[5]

The so-called Majority Text, edited by Zane Hodges and (the same) Arthur Farstad of Dallas Theological Seminary, was published in 1982. In the 'Preface' it is stated that this text is only of a provisional nature, implying that no-one can be sure yet that we actually have the entire Word of God, and also that the Word we do have may need to be amended in the future when more of the extant manuscripts have been collated and examined. To quote the exact words of Hodges and Farstad: 'It should therefore be kept in mind that the present work, *The Greek New Testament According to the Majority Text*, is both preliminary and provisional. It represents a first step...'.[6] Yet even as it is, this Majority Text contains nearly 1,900 changes to the Received Text, including the omission of such Scriptures as Matthew 27.35; Acts 8.37; 9.5,6; 10.6b; and 1 John 5.7.

It is no surprise therefore to find that in the marginal references of the NKJV New Testament there are approximately five hundred references to variant readings from the Majority Text, and a far higher number from the Critical Text. By their very existence these variant readings cast doubt on the very words of Holy Scripture and upon the doctrine of Divine Inspiration and Preservation. Furthermore, the integrity and accuracy of the Received Text, and by implication the Authorised Version itself, is hereby very seriously undermined. Dr James Price, the executive editor of the Old Testament section of the NKJV, admitted in an e-mail in April 1996, 'I am not a TR advocate. I happen to believe that God has preserved the autographic text in the whole body of evidence that He has preserved, not merely through the textual decisions of a committee of fallible men based on a handful of late manuscripts. The modern Critical Texts like NA26/27 [Nestles] and UBS [United Bible Societies] provide a list of the variations that have entered the manuscript traditions, and they provide the evidence that supports the different variants. In the apparatus they have left nothing out, the evidence is there. The apparatus indicates where possible additions, omissions, and alterations have occurred... I am not at war with the conservative modern versions [such as the New International Version and the New American Standard Version (sic)]'.[7]

Dr Price is suggesting here that the Received Text depends 'on a handful of late Greek manuscripts'. This is misleading, to say the very least. Frederick Nolan, in his *Inquiry into the Integrity of the Greek Vulgate or Received Text*, comments as follows: 'With respect to Manuscripts, it is indisputable that he [Erasmus] was acquainted with every variety which is known to us; having distributed them into two principal classes, one which corresponds with the Complutensian edition, the other with the Vatican manuscript [see Erasmus's *Preface to the New Testament*, 1546]. And he has specified the positive grounds on which he received the one and rejected the other'.[8] It is known that Erasmus collated and studied many manuscripts, observing thousands of variant readings including such as were found in Vaticanus (Codex B); and a friend called Bombasius, we are told, researched that for him. Certainly in his various editions of the Greek New Testament, his notes reveal that he was familiar with practically all the important variant readings known to modern scholars including Mark 16.9–20, Luke 22.43,44 and John 7.53–8.11.

Some Textual Critics, after B. F. Westcott and F. J. A. Hort, refer to 'families' of New Testament manuscripts. This again is misleading, as it is impossible to ascertain with any certainty the ancestors of manuscripts or to prove the exact relationship which one manuscript has to another. But the particular device of referring to 'families' enabled Westcott and Hort to dismiss the Traditional or Received Text, supported by 90% of the Greek manuscripts, as a mere descendant of an exceedingly corrupt ancestor! It is therefore much better to refer to 'text-types'. The major text-types are: the Traditional (Byzantine) text-type emanating from the Asia Minor/Greece area where Paul founded a number of churches (and called Byzantine because it was the recognised Greek text throughout the Byzantine period, AD 312–1453), and the Alexandrian text-type, associated with Alexandria and proceeding from Egypt. The Byzantine text-type has the overwhelming support of the Greek manuscripts (over 95% of the more than five thousand Greek manuscripts in existence); and naturally these have most impressive agreement among themselves. It is in this text-type that the Traditional Text has survived, which was published in the 16th and 17th centuries by Erasmus, Stephanus, Beza and the Elzevirs (Bonaventure and Abraham). In the 'Preface' to the Elzevirs' second edition (1633) reference is made to the 'text... now received by all' (*textum...nunc ab omnibus receptum*), from whence arose the designation 'Textus Receptus' or 'Received Text'. It is a text of this type which underlies the Authorised Version.

All of the existing New Testament Greek manuscripts are copies (apographs). None of the original writings of the Apostles (autographs) have survived. The Byzantine group of manuscripts are mostly, but by no means entirely, later copies. But some 4th-century manuscripts of the Alexandrian group have come to public notice since the publication of the Received Text in the 16th and 17th centuries. These are Codex Vaticanus (from the Vatican library) and Codex Sinaiticus (discovered in St. Catherine's Monastery on Mount Sinai in 1859). These manuscripts differ **radically** from the Traditional or Received Text. It is estimated that there are about six thousand differences. These include numerous omissions, sometimes of entire verses (e.g., Matthew 12.47, 18.11; Luke 17.36; Acts 28.29; Romans 15.24), and often even more than this (e.g., Matthew 16.2,3; Mark 9.44,46; John 5.3,4; Acts 24.6–8). Notorious among these, of course, are the last twelve verses of the Gospel of Mark and John 8.1–11. Even between themselves, these Alexandrian manuscripts show no agreement or consistency. H. C. Hoskier, after meticulously careful research, noted that in the four Gospels alone there were no less than three thousand differences between Codex Vaticanus and Codex Sinaiticus.

But since 1881 when, under the baleful influence of Westcott and Hort, the Revised Version of the Bible was published, the Alexandrian have been preferred to the Byzantine manuscripts chiefly because of their date, the view being that the oldest manuscripts are likely to be the most accurate. But this is a complete misconception, since accurate and approved copies would have been much in use and therefore would soon have become worn out – a damp climate not helping to preserve them as the arid climate of Egypt did with respect to the Alexandrian manuscripts. The good copies needed themselves to be copied and the evidence is that a great many copies were made in later centuries, a large number of which still exist today. It follows that, contrary to the footnotes in most modern versions, the 'oldest' are not at all likely to be the 'best' but could well be the 'worst'. Why? Because, recognised as defective, they were rejected and therefore little used.

Versions of the Bible since 1881 have been mainly based on these few early manuscripts. At first sight the NKJV appears to be an exception; yet while using the Received Text, it contains in its marginal references variant readings from these defective Alexandrian manuscripts. When examined, these marginal readings are seen to cast doubt on such fundamental doctrines as the Eternal Generation of the Son, the Union of Christ's Deity and Humanity, the Incarnation, the Blood Atonement, and the Eternal Conscious Punishment of the Wicked in Hell (e.g., John 1.18 – 'the only begotten Son' becomes 'the only begotten God'; 1 Corinthians 15.47 – omission of 'the Lord'; 1 Timothy 3.16 – 'God' changed to 'Who'; Colossians 1.14 – 'through his blood' is left out; Mark 9.46 – omission of 'Where their worm dieth not, and the fire is not quenched'). Here is a clear case of what the Scripture refers to in Ecclesiastes: 'Dead flies cause the ointment of the apothecary to send forth a stinking savour: *so doth* a little folly him that is in reputation for wisdom *and* honour' (10.1).

Even more serious is the fact that in the actual text of the NKJV New Testament there are a great many departures from the Received Text, where Critical Text readings have apparently been preferred and followed or other unwarranted changes have been made. This is a matter of gravest concern. Here are some examples:

■ John 10.6 – omission of the first instance of αὐτοις (*autois*), 'unto them' (AV: 'This parable spake Jesus unto them'; NKJV: 'Jesus used this illustration').

Autois is in all the Greek texts, both TR and Critical, and there is not even a textual variant indicated in the Critical editions; why the NKJV omits it is unclear.

■ Acts 15.23 – The NKJV omits ταδε (*tade*), 'after this manner', as does the Critical Text.

■ Acts 19.39 – The NKJV changes from the TR's περι ετερων (*peri heteron*), 'concerning other matters' to 'any other inquiry'. The Critical Text has περαιτερω (*peraitero*, 'further'). The NKJV reading is not just a change from plural to singular but appears to be based upon the use of the entirely different expression seen in the Critical Text.

■ Acts 27.14 – The NKJV omits κατ᾽ αὐτης (*kat' autes*), 'against it'; *kat autes* is in both the TR and the Critical Text. Again one is left to wonder why the NKJV omits it.

■ 2 Corinthians 4.14 – The NKJV changes δια Ἰησου (*dia Iesou*), 'by Jesus', to συν Ἰησου (*sun Iesou*), 'with Jesus', in keeping with the Critical Text reading – a very misleading change.

■ 2 John 7 – The NKJV changes from εἰσηλθον (*eiselthon*), 'entered into', to ἐξηλθον (*exelthon*), 'gone out into', the Critical Text reading.

■ Revelation 6.11 – The NKJV changes from the plural στολαι λευκαι (*stolai leukai*, 'white robes'), to the singular στολη λευκη (*stole leuke*) 'a white robe', which is the Critical Text reading.

In addition, there are some serious faults in the translation:

■ Matthew 15.32 – νηστεις (*nesteis*), 'fasting', is rendered 'hungry', losing the point that, in attending upon our Lord's ministry, the people had chosen to go without food (also changed in Mark 8.3).

■ Matthew 22.10 – ὁ γαμος (*ho gamos*), 'the wedding', is changed to 'the wedding hall'. Although hall appears in italics in the NKJV, it is an unnecessary addition unsupported by the Textus Receptus.

■ Luke 11.34 – ἁπλους (*haplous*), 'single', in the clause 'thine eye is single', wrongly becomes 'good', the true reference being to an eye that does not see double (also changed in Matthew 6.22);

■ Luke 11.54 – the words ἐκ του στοματος αὐτου (*ek tou stomatos autou*), 'out of his mouth' are changed to 'He might say', which does not translate the Greek.

9

- Luke 22.53 – οὐκ ἐξετείνατε τας χειρας ἐπ' ἐμε (*ouk exeteinate tas cheiras ep' eme*), 'ye stretched forth no hands against me', becomes 'you did not try to seize me' which is far from a literal translation.

- Acts 18.6 – ἀντιτασσομενων δε αὐτων (*antitassomenon de auton*), 'opposed themselves', that is, set themselves in the way to prevent the apostle preaching, is translated 'opposed him'.

- 2 Corinthians 7.2 – χωρησατε ἡμας (*choresate hemas*), 'receive us', is rendered 'open *your hearts* to us', as in the Revised Version; this is an example of dynamic equivalence.

- 2 Corinthians 11.29 – οὐκ ἐγω πυρουμαι (*ouk ego puroumai*), 'I burn not', is translated 'I do not burn with indignation', which is yet another case of interpretation rather than translation (the verb can be otherwise understood to mean 'burn with desire' or, perhaps, and preferably, 'burn with pain').

- Galatians 5.4 – the AV has 'Christ is become of no effect unto you'. In the NKJV, this is rendered 'You have become estranged from Christ'. The verb καταργεω (*katargeo*) literally means to render or make useless, or unprofitable, the idea being that those who sought justification by the law were severed from Christ and the benefits of His death. The NKJV unjustifiably imports the concept of a breakdown in the personal relationship with Christ, in place of the forfeiture of saving benefit.

- Philippians 3.8 – the things formerly relied upon which are now reckoned but σκυβαλα (*skubala*), 'dung' or 'muck', become merely 'rubbish' in the NKJV. However, the Greek word appears to be derived from one properly meaning human excrement, and thus conveys more literally something of the apostle's present estimate of, and aversion to, his Jewish legal privileges when considered a ground of justification (as is made clear in the AV).

- 1 Timothy 6.5 – νομιζοντων πορισμον εἰναι την εὐσεβειαν (*nomizonton porismon einai ten eusebeian*), literally 'supposing that gain is godliness', is rendered by the NKJV: 'who suppose that godliness is *a means of* gain'. Admittedly, in Greek it is possible to reverse the order of words when they are connected by a form of the verb 'to be', thus 'godliness is gain' just might be acceptable. However, regarding the words 'a means of', as indicated by the NKJV's use of italics and its omission of these words in the following verse, the inclusion of them here is invalid.

■ Hebrews 3.16 – in the NKJV is the mistranslation of ἀλλ' οὐ παντες (*all' ou pantes*), 'howbeit not all', to 'indeed, *was it* not all', thereby suggesting the rebellion of all the Israelites, whereas the truth was that Joshua and Caleb did not rebel.

■ Revelation 2.22 – 'sick' is added to κλινην (*klinen*), 'bed', making it 'sickbed'.

■ Revelation 16.16 – και συνηγαγεν αὐτους (*kai sunegagen autous*), 'And he gathered them together', is changed to 'And they gathered them together', effectively removing (without **any** manuscript support) God's sovereign action, and apparently attributing the action to unspecified malign forces.

It is therefore simply not true to say that the NKJV is faithful to the Received Text, nor is it true to say that it is a more accurate translation.

Headings

Mention could be made – and perhaps should be made – of the chapter and section headings in the NKJV, which are really very inferior to those found in our Authorised Version. Take the Song of Solomon, for example. The text is arbitrarily divided. To cite just one instance of this, half of 1.4 is said to have been spoken by 'the Shulamite' (identified in a marginal note as 'a Palestinian young woman') and the other half by 'the Daughters of Jerusalem'. Furthermore, the apportioning of the words to particular characters is novel and, we believe, highly questionable. Is it really the Shulamite who says, 'I *am* the rose of Sharon, *and* the lily of the valleys' in 2.1? It is not, according to the almost unanimous view of Reformed commentators who give a spiritual interpretation to this Song. We believe that these headings can only serve to mislead.

Pronouns

Another aspect of the NKJV is the abandonment of the use of the singular second person pronouns 'thee', 'thou' and 'thine' in preference for the more modern ambiguous 'you' and 'your'. The fact is that the former were not in common use in 1611, at the time of the translation of the Authorised Version. As early as the end of the 13th century, 'you' and 'your' had replaced them. But the AV translators were classical scholars and accuracy was uppermost in their minds; thus they retained the use of the singular pronouns when the original language texts required it. The use of 'you' and 'your' in the NKJV conceals the difference between the singular and plural in the second person pronouns of the classical languages. This is seen in the following verses:

■ Matthew 26.64 – 'Jesus saith unto him, Thou [the High Priest alone] hast said: nevertheless I say unto you [the people listening and all others], Hereafter shall ye see the Son of man sitting on the right hand of power, and coming in the clouds of heaven'.

■ Luke 22.31,32 – 'Satan hath desired *to have* you [all the disciples], that he may sift *you* as wheat: but I have prayed for thee [Peter], that thy faith fail not'.

■ John 3.7 – 'Marvel not that I said unto thee [Nicodemus], Ye [men and women generally] must be born again'.

There are in fact 14,500 uses of such pronouns in 10,500 verses of the Authorised Version. It cannot be said too strongly that 'thee', 'thou' and 'thine' are actually according to **Biblical** usage, based on the style of the Hebrew and Greek Scriptures, and have been used in the English-speaking world as a means of expressing reverence to God, particularly in prayer and praise. In this age of familiarity and lack of respect, the use of 'you' and 'your' in relation to the Most High God can indicate a lack of reverence. To a spiritually discerning ear, there is a vast difference between 'Thou art the Christ, the Son of the living God,' and 'You are the Christ...' (Matthew 16.16) – and this is not just a preference for the older word.

Greek Texts

The question must be asked, 'Has the Lord permitted His church to have an inaccurate Bible over all these centuries until the fairly recent discoveries of certain early Codices?' As already observed, it would appear that these early manuscripts have survived because they have not been much used. It is likely that they were judged inaccurate and defective, probably because they had been tampered with to suit the tenets of some heretical sect. Thus it is clear that God, in His special and mysterious Providence, has preserved the Holy Scriptures through the vast majority of manuscripts (mostly of the Byzantine school), copied and recopied carefully over many centuries, yet bearing a solid agreement and consistency one with another. That there are considerable and important differences between the few early Alexandrian Codices and the great majority of the Byzantine school of manuscripts is not in question, nor would anyone disagree that these differences have been incorporated into the printed Greek texts from which they are taken. Indeed, the Alexandrian-based Critical Texts and the Byzantine-based Textus Receptus differ in a number of significant passages.

The translators of the NKJV, while assuring their readers that they have translated from the Received Text, at the same time give in their marginal references and sometimes in the text itself equal credence to a Greek text which is wholly different from it. Once the position of the editors of this NKJV translation is known, it would appear that they have used the Received Text only as a means of paving the way for a substitution of the Authorised Version which would involve the introduction of their marginal variants into the main text of Scripture.

This translation, with its credence given to the marginal references, has the appearance of a most subtle attempt to discredit both the Received Text and the Authorised Version. The AV has been made such a blessing for many centuries, not only in our own country but throughout the English-speaking world. In many ways the NKJV is **far more dangerous** than the modern translations which have openly abandoned the Received Text in favour of texts built on the corrupt Alexandrian manuscripts.

Young People

We believe it is exceedingly simplistic and dangerous to put this new version into the hands of young people on the grounds that it is easier to understand. In reading it, they will not have an accurate translation of God's Word and the marginal notes will tend only to raise doubts in their minds regarding the variant readings. The plea some make, that they are only trying to make the Bible easier to read, is altogether inadmissible. It is essential that we pass on to others – especially to our young people – the **pure** Word of God, without any unfaithful and spurious additions. If we do not, suggesting that they might use the NKJV, those young people on reaching adulthood will almost certainly retain the use of this new version with which they have become familiar. The pressure will then be on our churches to adopt the Bible which many in the congregation seem to prefer. The Authorised Version could then, quite easily, be replaced.

Before such a time, any endorsement among us of the

NKJV will bring various other problems and evils. For example, once people begin to use a version which uses 'you' and 'your' in addressing God, it is only a matter of time before they lapse into this practice in public prayer, and then dissatisfaction will be found with the praise book because it retains the Scriptural and traditional usage. If, in naivety, we tolerate this new version, it is not difficult to foresee the time when the character of the testimony in our churches will radically change – and change for the worse. May our gracious God prevent this from ever happening.

Conclusion

For our part, we reject the New King James Version and we do not believe it should be used in our churches. The Authorised Version is far superior, and while not perfect it remains the best and most accurate English translation of God's Holy Word. Our prayer and hope is that those who have been deceived into thinking that the New King James Version represents a decided improvement and who have therefore introduced it into public worship, will realise that they have made a dreadful mistake and so restore to their churches the Authorised Version. As for the churches which continue to use the Authorised Version, we trust that it will remain in the hearts of their people and in their homes. We also trust that it will remain in the pulpits and pews of our churches.

May the Lord be pleased to bless and own our precious and beloved Authorised Version, to the good of our souls, the souls of our children, and the souls of our children's children.

Endnotes

1. Arthur L. Farstad, *The New King James Version: in the Great Tradition* (Nashville, TN, USA: Thomas Nelson, 1989), p. 34.

2. *Holy Bible: New King James Version* (Nashville, TN, USA: Thomas Nelson, 1982), pp. vi–vii.

3. It should be noted that editions of the New King James Version differ without note depending upon the year and country in which they were published. For example, the British editions, normally called the Revised Authorised Version (which are no longer published), do not capitalise pronouns referring to Deity.

4. *NKJV*, p. vi.

5. Ibid., p. vii.

6. Zane C. Hodges and Arthur L. Farstad, *The Greek New Testament According to the Majority Text* (Nashville, TN, USA: Thomas Nelson Publishers, 1982), p. x.

7. James Price, e-mail to David Cloud, April 30, 1996 in *The Bible Version Question/Answer Database* (Port Huron, MI, USA: Way of Life Literature, 2005), pp. 369–70.

8. Frederick Nolan, *An Inquiry into the Integrity of the Greek Vulgate, or Received Text of the New Testament* (London, England: F. C. and J. Rivington, 1815), pp. 413–414.